MW01505398

GUIDED BY SAINTS

Guided by Saints

A 30-Day Journal
for Inspiration and Direction

SUSAN HINES-BRIGGER

franciscan
media®
Cincinnati, Ohio

Biographies are adapted from SaintoftheDay.org.

Cover and book design by Mark Sullivan
ISBN 978-1-63253-396-8

Copyright ©2023 Susan Hines-Brigger
All rights reserved.

Published by Franciscan Media
28 W. Liberty St.
Cincinnati, OH 45202
www.FranciscanMedia.org

Printed in the United States of America.

Introduction

For Catholics, saints play an integral role in our faith—both in the Church and in our personal lives. We often look to their stories for inspiration and direction. Many times, though, it can be difficult to find a connection between their lives and ours. For that reason, they can seem unattainable and distant.

Most of us will never face the challenges or choices that many of the saints faced. But if we look a bit deeper into their lives, we start to realize that many of the situations or issues they faced are universal and timeless. In fact, many things they dealt with still challenge us in modern times.

As you work through this journal, I encourage you not only to read about the featured saints but also to put yourself in their place. What would you do in that situation? How would you feel or react? What can their story teach you in terms of your own life? How can you put their lessons into play today?

In these pages, you will discover that you are not as far removed from the saints as you think.

Find someplace quiet, grab a pen, and start to connect with the saints. You might be surprised how much you have in common with them.

"The secret of happiness is to live moment by moment and to thank God for all that He, in His goodness, sends to us day after day."

St. Gianna Beretta Molla

In less than forty years, Gianna Beretta Molla became a pediatric physician, a wife, a mother, and a saint!

She was born in Magenta, Italy, near Milano, the tenth of Alberto and Maria Beretta's thirteen children. An active member of the St. Vincent de Paul Society and a leader in the Catholic Action movement, Gianna also enjoyed skiing and mountain climbing. She earned degrees in medicine and surgery from the University of Pavia, eventually specializing in pediatrics. In 1952, Gianna opened a clinic in the small town of Mesero, where she met engineer Pietro Molla.

St. Gianna's feast day is April 19. She is the patron saint of doctors, unborn children, and wives.

Shortly before their 1955 marriage, Gianna wrote to Pietro: "Love is the most beautiful sentiment that the Lord has put into the soul of men and women." In the next four years, the Mollas had three children: Pierluigi, Mariolina, and Laura. The next two pregnancies ended in miscarriage.

Early in her final pregnancy, doctors discovered that Gianna had both a child and a tumor in her uterus. She allowed the surgeons to remove the tumor but not to perform the complete hysterectomy they recommended, which would have killed the child. Seven months later, in April 1962, Gianna Emanuela Molla was born at the hospital in Monza, but postoperative complications resulted in an infection for her mother. The following week Gianna Molla died at home and was buried in the cemetery of Mesero.

Gianna Emanuela went on to become a physician herself. Gianna Beretta Molla was beatified in 1994 and canonized ten years later. Her liturgical feast is celebrated on April 28.

From her letter to her husband, Pietro, we know how Gianna defined love. What is your description of love?

....

....

....

....

....

....

....

....

....

....

....

....

....

....

....

We have all faced difficult decisions at some point in our lives, whether big or small. In what ways did these experiences help to form who you are today?

In her profession, Gianna cared for others through her work as a pediatrician. Certainly, your life's vocation, whether in the workforce, at home, or in retirement, can serve as an opportunity to touch the lives of others. Reflect on some ways that you use your talents and skills to lift up the body of Christ.

"In God's will, there is great peace."

St. Josephine Bakhita

....

For many years, Josephine Bakhita was a slave, but her spirit was always free, and eventually that spirit prevailed.

Born in Olgossa in the Darfur region of southern Sudan, Josephine was kidnapped at the age of seven, sold into slavery, and given the name Bakhita, which means "fortunate." She was treated with brutality by her owners and resold several times. Finally, in 1883, she was sold to Callisto Legnani, Italian consul in Khartoum, Sudan.

Two years later, he took Josephine to Italy and gave her to his friend Augusto Michieli. Bakhita became babysitter to Mimmina Michieli, whom she accompanied to Venice's Institute of the Catechumens, run by the Canossian Sisters. While Mimmina was being instructed, Josephine felt drawn to the Catholic Church. She was baptized and confirmed in 1890, taking the name Josephine.

St. Josphine's feast day is February 8, also known as the World Day of Prayer, Reflection, and Action Against Human Trafficking.

When the Michielis returned to Africa and wanted to take Mimmina and Josephine back with them, the future saint refused to go. During the ensuing court case, the Canossian Sisters and the patriarch of Venice intervened on Josephine's behalf. The judge concluded that since slavery was illegal in Italy, she had actually been free since 1885.

Josephine entered the Institute of St. Magdalene of Canossa in 1893 and made her profession three years later. In 1902, she was transferred to the city of Schio (northeast of Verona), where she assisted her religious community through cooking, sewing, embroidery, and welcoming visitors. She soon became well loved by the children attending the sisters' school and the local citizens. She once said, "Be good, love the Lord, pray for those who do not know him. What a great grace it is to know God!"

The first steps toward her beatification began in 1959. She was beatified in 1992 and canonized eight years later.

....

Given what she endured, we would understand if St. Josephine had harbored anger and resentment toward those who enslaved her. She chose, however, to move beyond the hurts she had suffered and work to help others. What are some things in your life you are holding on to that are weighing on your heart?

....

....

....

....

....

....

....

....

Take some time to ponder why you are holding on to those experiences or emotions. What are you searching for that is keeping you from moving forward? Is it peace, acceptance, forgiveness?

Forgiveness does not mean forgetting what happened. Nor does it rely on input or participation from the other party in a situation. It is, rather, a personal gift to oneself. Write out what you would like to say to a person who has wronged you.

....

....

....

....

....

....

....

....

....

....

....

....

....

....

....

....

....

....

....

"Let us not tire of preaching love; it is the force that will overcome the world."

St. Oscar Arnulfo Romero

The night before he was murdered while celebrating Mass, Archbishop Oscar Romero of San Salvador said on the radio: "I would like to appeal in a special way to the men of the army, and in particular to the troops of the National Guard, the police, and the garrisons. Brothers, you belong to our own people. You kill your own brother peasants, and in the face of an order to kill that is given by a man, the law of God that says 'Do not kill!' should prevail.

"No soldier is obliged to obey an order counter to the law of God. No one has to comply with an immoral law. It is the time now that you recover your conscience and obey its dictates rather than the command of sin....Therefore, in the name of God, and in the name of this long-suffering people, whose laments rise to heaven every day more tumultuous, I beseech you, I beg you, I command you! In the name of God: 'Cease the repression!'"

St. Romero's feast day is March 24, the day he was assassinated while celebrating Mass.

Romero had eloquently upheld the Gospel— and effectively signed his own death warrant.

When he was appointed archbishop of San Salvador in 1977, Bishop Romero was considered a very "safe" choice. He had served as auxiliary bishop there for four years before his three years as bishop of Santiago de Maria.

Oscar's father wanted him to be a carpenter—a trade for which he demonstrated some talent. Seminary classes in El Salvador preceded his studies at Rome's Gregorian University and his ordination in 1942. After earning a doctorate in ascetical theology, he returned home and became a parish priest and later rector of an inter-diocesan seminary.

Three weeks after his appointment as archbishop, Romero was shaken by the murder of his good friend Jesuit Fr. Rutilio Grande, a vigorous defender of the rights of the poor. Five more priests were assassinated in the Archdiocese of San Salvador during Romero's years as its shepherd.

When a military junta seized control of the national government in 1979, Archbishop Romero publicly criticized the US government for backing the junta. His weekly radio sermons, broadcast throughout the country, were regarded by many as the most trustworthy source of news available.

Romero's funeral was celebrated in the plaza outside the cathedral and drew an estimated 250,000 mourners.

His tomb in the cathedral crypt soon drew thousands of visitors each year. On February 3, 2015, Pope Francis authorized a decree recognizing Oscar Romero as a martyr for the faith. His beatification took place in San Salvador on May 23, 2015, and he was canonized on October 14, 2018.

Is there anything that you care so deeply about that you would be willing to put your life at risk for it? What makes it so important to you?

....

....

....

....

....

....

....

....

....

If you had to make a decision between doing what is safe and doing what is right and just, which would you choose and why would you do so?

....

....

....

....

....

....
....
....
....
....
....

Archbishop Romero said, "I beseech you, I beg you, I command you! In the name of God: 'Cease the repression!'" There are many different forms of repression in society today, not just the military one he experienced. Think about some of those other types and reflect on what you think should be done to counter them.

....
....
....
....
....
....
....
....
....
....
....
....

"At all times and seasons, in every country and place, every day and all day, we must have a true and humble faith."

St. Francis of Assisi

The patron saint of Italy, Francis of Assisi was a poor little man who astounded and inspired the Church by taking the Gospel literally—not in a narrow, fundamentalist sense, but by actually following all that Jesus said and did, joyfully, without limit, and without a sense of self-importance.

Serious illness brought the young Francis to see the emptiness of his frolicking life as leader of Assisi's youth. Prayer—lengthy and difficult—led him to a self-emptying like that of Christ, climaxed by embracing a leper he met on the road. It symbolized his complete obedience to what he had heard in prayer: "Francis! Everything you have loved and desired in the flesh it is your duty to despise and hate, if you wish to know my will. And when you have begun this, all that now seems sweet and lovely to you will become intolerable and bitter, but all that you used to avoid will turn itself to great sweetness and exceeding joy."

St. Francis's feast day is Ocober 4. He is the patron saint of animals, ecology, messengers, and Italy.

From the cross in the neglected field-chapel of San Damiano, Christ told him, "Francis, go out and build up my house, for it is nearly falling down." Francis must have suspected a deeper meaning to "build up my house." But he would have been content for the rest of his life to be nothing but a poor laborer putting brick on brick to repair abandoned chapels. He gave up all his possessions, piling even his clothes before his earthly father, who was demanding restitution for Francis' "gifts" to the poor. He did this so he would be totally free to say, "Our Father in heaven." He was, for a time, considered to be a religious fanatic, begging from door to door when he could not get money for his work, evoking sadness or disgust in the hearts of his former friends, ridicule from the unthinking.

....

When Francis encountered the leper, he was hesitant to embrace him. What are some things in your life you're afraid to embrace but know you should?

....

....

....

....

....

....

....

....

....

....

....

....

....

....

Just as in Francis' time, our Church today is in need of rebuilding. What are some of the areas that you would like to see rebuilt? What are some ways you can be a part of that rebuilding process?

....

....

....

....

....

....

....

....

....

....

....

....

....

....

....

....

How much do you let the expectations and opinions of others limit your choices and actions in pursuit of a deeper faith life? What would it take for you to be as free as Francis?

"Let us always meet each other with a smile, for the smile is the beginning of love."

St. Teresa of Calcutta

Mother Teresa of Calcutta, the tiny woman recognized throughout the world for her work among the poorest of the poor, was beatified on October 19, 2003. Among those present were hundreds of Missionaries of Charity, the order she founded in 1950 as a diocesan religious community. Today the congregation also includes contemplative sisters and brothers and an order of priests.

Born to Albanian parents in what is now Skopje, Macedonia, Gonxha (Agnes) Bojaxhiu was the youngest of the three children who survived. For a time, the family lived comfortably, and her father's construction business thrived. But life changed overnight following his unexpected death.

During her years in public school, Agnes participated in a Catholic sodality and showed a strong interest in foreign missions. At age eighteen, she entered the Loreto Sisters of Dublin. It was 1928 when she said goodbye to her mother for the final time and made her way to a new land and a new life. The following year she was sent to the Loreto novitiate in Darjeeling, India. There she chose the name Teresa and prepared for a life of service.

St. Teresa's feast day is October 4, the day of her death. She is the patron saint of World Youth Day.

She was assigned to a high school for girls in Calcutta, where she taught history and geography to the daughters of the wealthy. But she could not escape the realities around her— the poverty, the suffering, the overwhelming numbers of destitute people.

In 1946, while riding a train to Darjeeling to make a retreat, Sister Teresa heard what she later explained as "a call within a call. The message was clear. I was to leave the convent and help the poor while living among them." She also heard a call to give up her life with the Sisters of Loreto and instead, to "follow Christ into the slums to serve him among the poorest of the poor."

After receiving permission to leave Loreto, establish a new religious community, and undertake her new work, Sister Teresa took a nursing course for several months. She returned to Calcutta, where she lived in the slums and opened a school for poor children. Dressed in a white sari and sandals—the ordinary dress of an Indian woman—she soon began getting to know her neighbors, many of them poor and sick.

The work was exhausting, but she was not alone for long. Volunteers who came to join her in the work, some of them former students, became the core of the Missionaries of Charity. Others helped by donating food, clothing, supplies, and the use of buildings. In 1952, the city of Calcutta gave Mother Teresa a former hostel, which became a home for the dying and the destitute. As the order expanded, services were also offered to orphans, abandoned children, alcoholics, the aging, and street people.

For the next four decades, Mother Teresa worked tirelessly on behalf of the poor. Her love knew no bounds. Nor did her energy, as she crisscrossed the globe pleading for support and inviting others to see the face of Jesus in the poorest of the poor. In 1979, she was awarded the Nobel Peace Prize. On September 5, 1997, God called her home. Bl. Teresa was canonized by Pope Francis on September 4, 2016.

When we think of Mother Teresa, chances are we immediately picture the sick and suffering on the poverty-ridden streets of Calcutta. But the heart of Mother Teresa's mission was caring for others. We might not be ministering to those in such dire circumstances, but caregiving is something we all do in one way or another. Perhaps you care for parents or children. Maybe your job entails caring for those in need. You might volunteer with an organization that helps those less fortunate.

Take some time to think about the ways in which you act as a caregiver in your life. How do those situations fulfill you?

....

....

....

....

....

....

....

As fulfilling as helping others can be, it can also be draining physically, mentally, and spiritually. Make a list of five ways you can refill yourself and your spirit.

....

....

....

....

....

....

....

....

It is well-documented that Mother Teresa suffered a "dark
night of the soul" during her life, an extremely difficult or
painful period. Reflect on your own life and some of the dark
times you have experienced. Write your memories of those
times and try to remember what helped you get through
them.

....

....

....

....

....

....

....

....

....

....

....

....

"We become what we love and who we love shapes what we become."

St. Clare of Assisi

A popular movie made about Francis of Assisi portrays Clare as a golden-haired beauty following Francis through sun-drenched fields. While this reduces her role to muse and supporting actress, the beginning of her religious life was indeed movie material. Having refused to marry at fifteen, Clare was moved by the dynamic preaching of Francis. At eighteen, she escaped from her father's home one night, was met on the road by friars carrying torches, and in the poor little chapel called the Portiuncula received a rough woolen habit, exchanged her jeweled belt for a rope with knots in it, and sacrificed her long tresses to Francis's scissors. He placed her in a Benedictine convent, which her father and uncles immediately stormed in rage. Clare clung to the altar of the church, threw aside her veil to show her cropped hair, and remained adamant.

St. Clare's feast day is August 11, marking the day she died. She is the patron saint of television and protection from eye disorders.

Sixteen days later, her sister Agnes joined her. Others followed. They lived a simple life of great poverty, austerity, and complete seclusion from the world, according to a Rule which Francis gave them as a Second Order. Francis was Clare's lifelong friend and spiritual guide. When she was twenty-one, Francis obliged Clare under obedience to accept the office of abbess, which she exercised until her death. Under her leadership, the greatest emphasis for the Poor Ladies, as they were called, was on Gospel poverty. They possessed no property, even in common, subsisting on daily contributions. When even the pope tried to persuade Clare to mitigate this practice, she showed her characteristic firmness: "I need to be absolved from my sins, but I do not wish to be absolved from the obligation of following Jesus Christ."

....

Clare was a very strong woman, both in her life and devotion. Each of us is strong in our own ways. Make a list of what you think are your strongest traits.

....

....

....

....

....

....

....

....

....

....

....

....

....

....

....

....

Francis and Clare had a close relationship. Think about who in your life serves as faithful companions to you. What is it that makes them such good friends?

....

....

....

....

....

....

....

....

....

....

....

....

....

....

....

St. Clare held on to life until she knew her rule for the sisters had been approved by Rome. What would you like your legacy to be?

....

....

....

....

....

....

....

....

....

....

....

....

....

....

....

....

"Take every day as a ring which you must engrave, adorn, and embellish with your actions, to be offered up in the evening at the altar of God."

St. Elizabeth Ann Seton

Mother Seton is one of the keystones of the American Catholic Church. She founded the first American religious community for women, the Sisters of Charity. She opened the first American parish school and established the first American Catholic orphanage. All this she did in the span of forty-six years while raising her children.

Elizabeth Ann Bayley Seton is a true daughter of the American Revolution, born August 28, 1774, just two years before the Declaration of Independence. By birth and marriage, she was linked to the first families of New York and enjoyed the fruits of high society. Reared a staunch Episcopalian, she learned the value of prayer, Scripture, and a nightly examination of conscience. Her father, Dr. Richard Bayley, did not have much use for churches but was a great humanitarian, teaching his daughter to love and serve others.

The feast day of St. Elizabeth Ann Seton, patron of Catholic schools and widows, is on January 4.

The early deaths of her mother in 1777 and her baby sister in 1778 gave Elizabeth a feel for eternity and the temporary nature of this pilgrim life on earth. Far from brooding and being sullen, she faced each new "holocaust," as she put it, with hopeful cheerfulness.

At nineteen, Elizabeth was the belle of New York and married a handsome, wealthy businessman, William Magee Seton. They had five children before his business failed and he died of tuberculosis.

At thirty, Elizabeth was widowed and penniless with a family to support.

While in Italy with her dying husband, Elizabeth witnessed Catholicity in action through family friends. Three basic points led her to become a Catholic: belief in the Real Presence, devotion to the Blessed Mother, and conviction that the Catholic Church stretched back to the apostles and to Christ. Many of her family and friends rejected her when she became a Catholic in March 1805.

To support her children, she opened a school in Baltimore. From the beginning, her group of teachers followed the structure of a religious community, which Elizabeth officially founded in 1809.

In more than a thousand letters written by Mother Seton, we see the development of her spiritual life from ordinary goodness to heroic sanctity. She suffered great trials of sickness, misunderstanding, the death of loved ones, and the heartache of a wayward son. She died January 4, 1821 and became the first American-born citizen to be beatified (1963) and then canonized (1975). She is buried in Emmitsburg, Maryland.

....

Though she was faced with many losses in her life, Elizabeth is said to have faced them with "hopeful cheerfulness." Make a list of five trying events you have experienced in your life. Then make a list of ten blessings you have received.

....

....

....

....

....

....

....

....

....

....

Think of three things about the Catholic faith that are
important to you. Reflect on what it is about those aspects
that speak to you so strongly.

....

....

....

....

....

....

....

....

....

....

....

....

....

....

Raising five children on her own had to be extremely stressful and exhausting for Elizabeth. While it may be for very different reasons, stress is something many of us understand all too well. Take a moment to close your eyes and take some deep breaths. Write your own prayer for dealing with stress.

"I would write a thousand foolish things that one might be to the point, if only it might make us praise God more."

St. Teresa of Avila

The sixteenth century was an age of exploration as well as political, social, and religious upheaval. Teresa lived in a time of turmoil and reform. She was born before the Protestant Reformation and died almost twenty years after the closing of the Council of Trent.

God's gift to Teresa in and through which she became holy and left her mark on the Church and the world is threefold: She was a woman, she was a contemplative, and she was an active reformer.

As a woman, Teresa stood on her own two feet, even in the man's world of her time. She was "her own woman," entering the Carmelites despite strong opposition from her father. She is a person wrapped not so much in silence as in mystery. Beautiful, talented, outgoing, adaptable, affectionate, courageous, enthusiastic, she was totally human. Like Jesus, she was a mystery of paradoxes: wise yet practical; intelligent yet much in tune with her experience; a mystic yet an energetic reformer; a holy woman yet a womanly woman.

October 15 is the feast day of St. Teresa. She is the patron saint of relief from headaches.

Teresa was a woman "for God"—a woman of prayer, discipline, and compassion. Her heart belonged to God. Her ongoing conversion was an arduous, lifelong struggle, involving ongoing purification and suffering. She was misunderstood, misjudged, and opposed in her efforts at reform. Yet she carried on, courageous and faithful;

she also struggled with a sense of mediocrity, illness, and external opposition. In the midst of all this, she clung to God in life and in prayer. Her writings on prayer and contemplation are drawn from her experience: powerful, practical, and graceful.

Teresa was a woman "for others." Though a contemplative, she spent much of her time and energy seeking to reform herself and the Carmelites, to lead them back to the full observance of the primitive Rule. She founded more than a half-dozen new monasteries. She traveled, wrote, fought—always to renew, to reform. In herself, in her prayer, in her life, in her efforts to reform, and in all the people she touched, she was a woman who inspired and gave life.

Her writings, especially *The Way of Perfection* and *The Interior Castle*, have helped generations of believers. In 1970, the Church gave her the title she had long held in the popular mind: Doctor of the Church. She and St. Catherine of Siena were the first women to be so honored.

....

At some point or another, you probably were misunderstood or misjudged for something you did or believed. How did that make you feel and how did you handle it?

....

....

....

....

....

....

....

....

....

In *The Interior Castle,* St. Teresa describes the journey of faith as having seven mansions or dwelling places. Find a summary of her description and then spend some time reflecting and writing about what you think she meant.

....

....

....

....

....

....

....

....

....

....

....

....

....

St. Teresa was always working for renewal and reform, both in the world and in herself. Think of some ways that you can renew yourself and your faith life.

"It is a lesson we all need - to let alone the things that do not concern us. He has other ways for others to follow Him; all do not go by the same path."

St. Katharine Drexel

If your father is an international banker and you ride in a private railroad car, you are not likely to be drawn into a life of voluntary poverty. But if your mother opens your home to the poor three days each week and your father spends half an hour each evening in prayer, it is not impossible that you will devote your life to the poor and give away millions of dollars. Katharine Drexel did that.

Born in Philadelphia in 1858, she had an excellent education and traveled widely. As a rich girl, Katharine also had a grand debut into society. But when she nursed her stepmother through a three-year terminal illness, she saw that all the Drexel money could not buy safety from pain or death, and her life took a profound turn.

St. Katharine died on March 3, which is now her feast day. She is the patron saint of racial justice and philanthropists.

Katharine had always been interested in the plight of the indigenous peoples, having been appalled by what she read in Helen Hunt Jackson's *A Century of Dishonor*. While on a European tour, she met Pope Leo XIII and asked him to send more missionaries to Wyoming for her friend Bishop James O'Connor. The pope replied, "Why don't you become a missionary?" His answer shocked her into considering new possibilities.

Back home, Katharine visited the Dakotas, met the Sioux leader Red Cloud, and began her systematic aid to native missions.

Katharine Drexel could easily have married. But after much discussion with Bishop O'Connor, she wrote in 1889, "The feast of St. Joseph brought me the grace to give the remainder of my life to the Indians and the Colored." Newspaper headlines screamed, "Gives Up Seven Million!"

After three-and-a-half years of training, Mother Drexel and her first band of nuns—Sisters of the Blessed Sacrament for Indians and Colored—opened a boarding school in Santa Fe. A string of foundations followed. By 1942, she had a system of Black Catholic schools in thirteen states, plus forty mission centers and twenty-three rural schools. Segregationists harassed her work, even burning a school in Pennsylvania. In all, she established fifty missions for Indians in sixteen states.

Two saints met when Mother Drexel was advised by Mother Cabrini about the "politics" of getting her order's Rule approved in Rome. Her crowning achievement was the founding of Xavier University in New Orleans, the first Catholic university in the United States for African Americans.

At seventy-seven, Mother Drexel suffered a heart attack and was forced to retire. Apparently her life was over. But then came almost twenty years of quiet, intense prayer from a small room overlooking the sanctuary. Small notebooks and slips of paper record her various prayers, ceaseless aspirations, and meditations. She died at ninety-six and was canonized in 2000.

What does the concept of poverty mean to you? Is it just a
lack of material goods or can it be something deeper?

....

....

....

....

....

....

....

....

Imagine that you have millions of dollars to donate to
various charities. Make a list of ones you would support
and why you would do so. What does your list tell you about
yourself?

....

....

....

....

....

....

....

....

....

....

Katharine had determination and resiliency in carrying
out her work. Think back to times when you feel you have
exhibited those qualities in your own life. How did these
times make you feel?

....

....

....

....

....

....

....

....

....

....

....

....

....

....

....

....

....

"For the love of Jesus, I forgive Alessandro...and I want him to be with me in paradise."

St. Maria Goretti

One of the largest crowds ever assembled for a canonization—250,000—symbolized the reaction of millions touched by the simple story of Maria Goretti. She was the daughter of a poor Italian tenant farmer, had no chance to go to school, and never learned to read or write. When Maria made her First Communion not long before her death, she was one of the larger and somewhat backward members of the class.

On a hot afternoon in July, Maria was sitting at the top of the stairs of her house, mending a shirt. She was not quite twelve years old, but physically mature. A cart stopped outside, and a neighbor, eighteen-year-old Alessandro, ran up the stairs. He seized her and pulled her into a bedroom. She struggled and tried to call for help. "No, God does not wish it," she cried out. "It is a sin. You would go to hell for it." Alessandro began striking at her blindly with a long dagger.

St. Maria's feast day is July 6, the day she died, just one day after she was attacked. She is the patron saint of girls.

Maria was taken to a hospital. Her last hours were marked by the simple compassion of the good—concern about where her mother would sleep, forgiveness of her murderer (she had been in fear of him but did not say anything lest she cause trouble to his family), and her devout welcoming of the Viaticum, her last Holy Communion. She died about twenty-four hours after the attack.

Alessandro was sentenced to thirty years in prison. For a long time he was unrepentant and surly. One night he had a dream, or vision, of Maria gathering flowers and offering them to him. His life changed. When he was released after twenty-seven years, his first act was to beg the forgiveness of Maria's mother.

Devotion to the young martyr grew, miracles were worked, and in less than half a century she was canonized. At her beatification in 1947, her eighty-two-year-old mother, two sisters, and her brother appeared with Pope Pius XII on the balcony of St. Peter's. Three years later, at Maria's canonization, a sixty-six-year-old Alessandro Serenelli knelt among the quarter-million people and cried tears of joy.

....

When you read Maria's story, it's easy to think immediately of revenge. Are there people in your life for whom you hold a grudge or wish ill will toward? If so, how does holding that emotion in your heart affect you?

....

....

....

....

....

....

....

....

....

Reflect on the concept of forgiveness and its power.

....

Are there things for which you need to forgive yourself?

....

....

....

....

....

....

....

....

....

....

....

....

....

....

....

....

....

....

"I would like to take that man's place."

St. Maximilian Mary Kolbe

....

"I don't know what's going to become of you!" How many parents have said that? Maximilian Mary Kolbe's reaction was, "I prayed very hard to Our Lady to tell me what would happen to me. She appeared, holding in her hands two crowns, one white, one red. She asked if I would like to have them—one was for purity, the other for martyrdom. I said, 'I choose both.' She smiled and disappeared." After that he was not the same.

He entered the minor seminary of the Conventual Franciscans in Lvív—then Poland, now Ukraine—near his birthplace, and at sixteen he became a novice. Though Maximilian later achieved doctorates in philosophy and theology, he was deeply interested in science, even drawing plans for rocket ships.

Ordained at age twenty-four, Maximilian saw religious indifference as the deadliest poison of the day. His mission was to combat it. He had already founded the Militia of the Immaculata, whose aim was to fight evil with the witness of the good life, prayer, work, and suffering. He dreamed of and then founded *Knight of the Immaculata*, a religious magazine under Mary's protection to preach the Good News to all nations. For the work of publication, he established a "City of the Immaculata"—Niepokalanow—that housed seven hundred of his Franciscan brothers. He later founded another one in Nagasaki, Japan. Both the Militia and the magazine ultimately reached the one-million

St. Maximilian Mary Kolbe's feast day is August 14, marking the day he died in a Nazi concentration camp.

mark in members and subscribers. His love of God was daily filtered through devotion to Mary.

In 1939, the Nazi panzers overran Poland with deadly speed. Niepokalanow was severely bombed. Kolbe and his friars were arrested, then released in less than three months, on the feast of the Immaculate Conception.

In 1941, Fr. Kolbe was arrested again. The Nazis' purpose was to liquidate the select ones, the leaders. The end came quickly, three months later in Auschwitz, after terrible beatings and humiliations.

A prisoner had escaped. The commandant announced that ten men would die. He relished walking along the ranks. "This one. That one."

As they were being marched away to the starvation bunkers, Number 16670 dared to step from the line.

"I would like to take that man's place. He has a wife and children."
"Who are you?"
"A priest."

No name, no mention of fame. Silence. The commandant, dumbfounded, perhaps with a fleeting thought of history, kicked Sergeant Francis Gajowniczek out of line and ordered Fr. Kolbe to go with the nine. In the "block of death" they were ordered to strip naked, and their slow starvation began in darkness. But there was no screaming—the prisoners sang. By the eve of the Assumption, four were left alive. The jailer came to finish Kolbe off as he sat in a corner praying. He lifted his fleshless arm to receive the bite of the hypodermic needle. It was filled with carbolic acid. They burned his body with all the others. Fr. Kolbe was beatified in 1971 and canonized in 1982.

Think about the difficult or challenging moments in your life. How did your reaction to those situations shape who you are?

....

....

....

....

....

....

....

....

Write a prayer for all those affected by war. Include it in your daily prayers.

....

....

....

....

....

....

....

....

....

....

....

Reflect on the theme of war as a pro-life issue.

....

....

....

....

....

....

....

....

....

....

....

....

....

....

....

....

....

....

....

"St. Joseph did not do extraordinary things, but rather by the constant practice of ordinary and common virtues, he attained that sanctity which elevates him above all the other saints."—St. Joseph Marello

St. Joseph, Husband of Mary

The Bible pays Joseph the highest compliment: He was a "just" man. When the Bible speaks of God "justifying" someone, it means that God, the all-holy or "righteous" one, so transforms a person that the individual shares somehow in God's own holiness, and hence it is really "right" for God to love him or her. In other words, God is not playing games, acting as if we were lovable when we are not.

By saying Joseph was "just," the Bible means that he was one who was completely open to all that God wanted to do for him. He became holy by opening himself totally to God. It is no contradiction of Joseph's holiness that he decided to divorce Mary when she was found to be with child. The important words of the Bible are that he planned to do this "quietly" because he was "a righteous man, yet unwilling to expose her to shame" (Matthew 1:19).

St. Joseph's feast day is celebrated on March 19. He is the patron saint of carpenters and families.

The just man was simply, joyfully, wholeheartedly obedient to God—in marrying Mary, in naming Jesus, in shepherding the precious pair to Egypt, in bringing them to Nazareth, in the undetermined number of years of quiet faith and courage.

Do you consider yourself "just?" If so, what do you mean by that?

Though Joseph is a major figure in the story of our faith, he is not a very prominent one in the Bible. Are there any times you have felt lost in the shadows?

Joseph was a good man. Think of some of the good
and honorable men in your life. Let them know how
you feel.

"Miss no single opportunity of making some small sacrifice, here by a smiling look, there by a kindly word; always doing the smallest right and doing it all for love."

St. Thérèse of Lisieux

"I prefer the monotony of obscure sacrifice to all ecstasies. To pick up a pin for love can convert a soul."

These are the words of Thérèse of Lisieux, a Carmelite nun called the "Little Flower," who lived a cloistered life of obscurity in the convent of Lisieux, France. And her preference for hidden sacrifice did indeed convert souls. Few saints of God are more popular than this young nun. Her autobiography, *The Story of a Soul*, is read and loved throughout the world. Thérèse Martin entered the convent at the age of fifteen and died in 1897 at the age of twenty-four.

Life in a Carmelite convent is indeed uneventful and consists mainly of prayer and hard domestic work. But Thérèse possessed that holy insight that redeems the time, however dull that time may be. She saw in quiet suffering a redemptive suffering, suffering that was indeed her apostolate. Thérèse said she came to the Carmel convent "to save souls and pray for priests." And shortly before she died, she wrote: "I want to spend my heaven doing good on earth."

St. Thérèse's feast day is October 1. She is the patron saint of florists, pilots, and priests.

Thérèse was canonized in 1925. On October 19, 1997, Pope John Paul II proclaimed her a Doctor of the Church, the third woman to be so recognized in light of her holiness and the influence of her teaching on spirituality in the Church.

Her parents, Louis and Zélie Martin, were beatified in 2008 and canonized in 2015.

....

St. Thérèse is known for doing good in little ways. Make a list of ideas for small ways you can brighten someone else's day. Then do one of those things every day for a week.

....

....

....

....

....

....

....

....

....

....

....

....

....

....

....

....

Flowers, especially roses, are often associated with St. Thérèse. Decorate this page with flowers in her honor. You can draw and color them yourself, decorate with stickers, or use other art supplies.

Reflect on this quote from St. Thérèse: "If I did not simply live from one moment to another, it would be impossible for me to be patient, but I only look at the present, I forget the past, and I take good care not to forestall the future."

"Consult not your fears but your hopes and your dreams."

St. John XXIII

Although few people had as great an impact on the twentieth-century Church as Pope John XXIII, he avoided the limelight as much as possible. Indeed, one writer has noted that his "ordinariness" seems one of his most remarkable qualities.

The firstborn son of a farming family in Sotto il Monte, near Bergamo in northern Italy, Angelo Giuseppe Roncalli was always proud of his down-to-earth roots. In Bergamo's diocesan seminary, he joined the Secular Franciscan Order.

After his ordination in 1904, Fr. Roncalli returned to Rome for canon law studies. He soon worked as his bishop's secretary, Church history teacher in the seminary, and publisher of the diocesan paper.

St. John XXIII's feast day is October 11, marking the opening date of the Second Vatican Council in 1962.

His service as a stretcher-bearer for the Italian army during World War I gave him a firsthand knowledge of war. In 1921, Fr. Roncalli was made national director in Italy of the Society for the Propagation of the Faith. He also found time to teach patristics at a seminary in the Eternal City.

In 1925, he became a papal diplomat, serving first in Bulgaria, then in Turkey, and finally in France. During World War II, he became well acquainted with Orthodox Church leaders. With the help of Germany's ambassador to Turkey, Archbishop Roncalli helped save an estimated 24,000 Jewish people.

Named a cardinal and appointed patriarch of Venice in 1953, he was finally a residential bishop. A month short of entering his seventy-eighth year, Cardinal Roncalli was elected pope, taking the name John after his father and John the Baptist and John the Evangelist, the two patrons of Rome's cathedral known as St. John Lateran. Pope John took his work very seriously but not himself. His wit soon became proverbial, and he began meeting with political and religious leaders from around the world. In 1962, he was deeply involved in efforts to resolve the Cuban missile crisis.

His most famous encyclicals were *Mother and Teacher* (1961) and *Peace on Earth* (1963). Pope John XXIII enlarged the membership in the College of Cardinals and made it more international. In his address at the opening of the Second Vatican Council, he criticized the "prophets of doom" who "in these modern times see nothing but prevarication and ruin." Pope John XXIII set a tone for the Council when he said, "The Church has always opposed...errors. Nowadays, however, the Spouse of Christ prefers to make use of the medicine of mercy rather than that of severity."

On his deathbed, Pope John said: "It is not that the gospel has changed; it is that we have begun to understand it better. Those who have lived as long as I have...were enabled to compare different cultures and traditions, and know that the moment has come to discern the signs of the times, to seize the opportunity and to look far ahead."

"Good Pope John" died on June 3, 1963. St. John Paul II beatified him in 2000, and Pope Francis canonized him in 2014.

St. John Paul XXIII introduced a major shift in the Church when he opened Vatican II. If you could change something within the Church, what would you change and why?

....

....

....

....

....

....

....

....

Change in our lives can be difficult. Reflect on some of the major changes in your life and what you've learned about yourself from them.

....

....

....

....

....

....

....

....

John Paul XXIII was well known for his wit and joy. Make a
list of things that bring you joy.

....

....

....

....

....

....

....

....

....

....

....

....

....

....

....

....

....

"Hope comes from love, because people always trust in those they love."

St. Catherine of Siena

Catherine made complete surrender to Christ the central value in her short life; it sounds clearly and consistently through her experience. What is most impressive about her is that she learns to view her surrender to her Lord as a goal to be reached through time.

She was the twenty-third child of Jacopo and Lapa Benincasa and grew up as an intelligent, cheerful, and intensely religious person. Catherine disappointed her mother by cutting off her hair as a protest against being overly encouraged to improve her appearance in order to attract a husband. Her father ordered her to be left in peace, and she was given a room of her own for prayer and meditation.

She entered the Dominican Third Order at eighteen and spent the next three years in seclusion, prayer, and austerity. Gradually, a group of followers gathered around her—men and women, priests and religious. An active public apostolate grew out of her contemplative life. Her letters, mostly for spiritual instruction and encouragement of her followers, began to take more and more note of public affairs. Opposition and slander resulted from her mixing fearlessly with the world and speaking with the candor and authority of one completely committed to Christ. She was cleared of all charges at the Dominican General Chapter of 1374.

St. Catherine's feast day is April 29. She is the patron saint of Europe, fire prevention, and Italy.

Her public influence reached great heights because of her evident holiness, her membership in the Dominican Third Order, and the deep impression she made on the pope. She worked tirelessly for the crusade against the Turks and for peace between Florence and the pope.

In 1378, the Great Schism began, splitting the allegiance of Christendom between two, then three, popes and putting even saints on opposing sides. Catherine spent the last two years of her life in Rome, in prayer and pleading on behalf of the cause of Pope Urban VI and the unity of the Church. She offered herself as a victim for the Church in its agony. She died surrounded by her "children" and was canonized in 1461.

Catherine ranks high among the mystics and spiritual writers of the Church. In 1939, she and Francis of Assisi were declared co-patrons of Italy. Pope Paul VI named her and Teresa of Avila doctors of the Church in 1970. Her spiritual testament is found in *The Dialogue*.

When have you felt you disappointed someone? Could you have done something differently? Why or why not?

In the spirit of St. Catherine, write letters regarding issues you care about to those who can facilitate change.

....

During her life, Catherine worked for the cause of peace.
What can you do to help bring about peace, even on a small
scale?

....

....

....

....

....

....

....

....

....

....

....

....

....

....

....

....

....

....

"I was born for this."

St. Joan of Arc

....

Burned at the stake as a heretic after a politically motivated trial, Joan was beatified in 1909 and canonized in 1920.

Born of a fairly well-to-do peasant couple in Domremy-Greux, southeast of Paris, Joan was only twelve when she experienced a vision and heard voices that she later identified as Sts. Michael the Archangel, Catherine of Alexandria, and Margaret of Antioch.

During the Hundred Years War, Joan led French troops against the English and recaptured the cities of Orléans and Troyes. This enabled Charles VII to be crowned as king in Reims in 1429. Captured near Compiegne the following year, Joan was sold to the English and placed on trial for heresy and witchcraft. Professors at the University of Paris supported Bishop Pierre Cauchon of Beauvis, the judge at her trial; Cardinal Henry Beaufort of Winchester, England, participated in the questioning of Joan in prison. In the end, she was condemned for wearing men's clothes. The English resented France's military success—to which Joan contributed.

St. Joan's feast day is May 8. She is the patron saint of France and military members.

On May 30, 1431, Joan was burned at the stake in Rouen, and her ashes were scattered in the Seine River. A second Church trial twenty-five years later nullified the earlier verdict, which was reached under political pressure.

Remembered by most people for her military exploits, Joan had a great love for the sacraments, which strengthened her compassion toward the poor. Popular devotion to her increased greatly in nineteenth-century France and later among French soldiers during World War I. Theologian George Tavard writes that her life "offers a perfect example of the conjunction of contemplation and action" because her spiritual insight is that there should be a "unity of heaven and earth."

....

What do you think can be done about the current state of politics?

....

....

....

....

....

....

....

....

....

....

....

....

....

....

....

What is one message you want to share with the world?

The story of Joan brings up a variety of topics, such as war, execution, justice, and even gender issues. Take some time to reflect on your feelings about these topics.

"In the twilight of our life, we shall be judged according to love."

St. Aloysius Gonzaga

....

The Lord can make saints anywhere, even amid the brutality and license of Renaissance life. The city of Florence was the "mother of piety" for Aloysius Gonzaga despite his exposure to a "society of fraud, dagger, poison, and lust." As a son of a princely family, he grew up in royal courts and army camps. His father wanted Aloysius to be a military hero.

At age seven, Aloysius experienced a profound spiritual quickening. His prayers included the Office of Mary, the psalms, and other devotions. At age nine, he came from his hometown of Castiglione to Florence to be educated; by age eleven, he was teaching catechism to poor children, fasting three days a week, and practicing great austerities. When he was thirteen years old, he traveled with his parents and the Empress of Austria to Spain and acted as a page in the court of Philip II. The more Aloysius saw of court life, the more disillusioned he became and the more he sought relief in learning about the lives of saints.

St. Aloysius' feast is celebrated on June 21. He is the patron saint of teenagers and seminarians.

A book about the experience of Jesuit missionaries in India suggested to him the idea of entering the Society of Jesus, and in Spain his decision became final. Now began a four-year contest with his father. Eminent churchmen and laypeople were pressed into service to persuade Aloysius to remain in his "normal" vocation. Finally he prevailed, was allowed to renounce his right to succession, and was received into the Jesuit novitiate.

Like other seminarians, Aloysius was faced with a new kind of penance—that of accepting different ideas about the exact nature of penance. He was obliged to eat more and to take recreation with the other students. He was forbidden to pray except at stated times. He spent four years in the study of philosophy and had St. Robert Bellarmine as his spiritual adviser.

In 1591, a plague struck Rome. The Jesuits opened a hospital of their own. The superior general himself and many other Jesuits rendered personal service. Because he nursed patients, washing them and making their beds, Aloysius caught the disease. A fever persisted after his recovery, and he was so weak he could scarcely rise from bed. Yet he maintained his great discipline of prayer, knowing that he would die three months later within the octave of Corpus Christi, at the age of twenty-three.

The sacraments played an important role in St. Aloysius' life. What do the sacraments mean to you?

Have you ever been burdened with expectations that don't align with your personal desires? How did you address it? What did you learn?

What would you do if you knew being of service to others
might result in your death?

"God has arranged all things in the world in consideration of everything else."

St. Hildegard of Bingen

Abbess, artist, author, composer, mystic, pharmacist, poet, preacher, theologian—where to begin in describing this remarkable woman?

Born into a noble family, she was instructed for ten years by the holy woman Bl. Jutta. When Hildegard was eighteen, she became a Benedictine nun at the Monastery of Saint Disibodenberg. Ordered by her confessor to write down the visions she had received since the age of three, Hildegard took ten years to write her *Scivias* ("Know the Ways"). Pope Eugene III read it, and in 1147 he encouraged her to continue writing. Her *Book of the Merits of Life* and *Book of Divine Works* followed. She wrote more than 300 letters to people who sought her advice; she also composed short works on medicine and physiology and sought advice from contemporaries such as St. Bernard of Clairvaux.

The feast of St. Hildegard on September 17 marks the day of her death.

Hildegard's visions caused her to see humans as "living sparks" of God's love, coming from God as daylight comes from the sun. Sin destroyed the original harmony of creation; Christ's redeeming death and Resurrection opened up new possibilities. Virtuous living reduces the estrangement from God and others that sin causes.

Like all mystics, Hildegard saw the harmony of God's creation and the place of women and men in that. This unity was not apparent to many of her contemporaries.

Hildegard was no stranger to controversy. The monks near her original foundation protested vigorously when she moved her monastery to Bingen, overlooking the Rhine River. She confronted Emperor Frederick Barbarossa for supporting at least three antipopes. Hildegard also challenged the Cathars, who rejected the Catholic Church and claimed to follow a more pure Christianity.

Between 1152 and 1162, Hildegard often preached in the Rhineland. Her monastery was placed under interdict because she had permitted the burial of a young man who had been excommunicated. She insisted that he had been reconciled with the Church and had received its sacraments before dying. Hildegard protested bitterly when the local bishop forbade the celebration or reception of the Eucharist at the Bingen monastery, a sanction that was lifted only a few months before her death.

In 2012, Hildegard was canonized and named a Doctor of the Church by Pope Benedict XVI. Her liturgical feast is celebrated on September 17.

....

Each of us has many different facets to our lives. How would you describe yourself if someone asked?

....

....

....

....

....

....

....

....

What are some of the characteristics of Hildegard that most resonate with you?

....

....

....

....

....

....

....

....

....

....

....

....

....

....

....

If you were to write letters to people offering them advice, as Hildegard did, what would you say?

"Always forward, never back."

St. Junipero Serra

In 1776, when the American Revolution was beginning in the east, another part of the future United States was being born in California. That year, a gray-robed Franciscan founded Mission San Juan Capistrano, now famous for its annually returning swallows. San Juan was the seventh of nine missions established under the direction of this indomitable Spaniard.

Born on Spain's island of Mallorca, Serra entered the Franciscan Order and took the name of St. Francis' childlike companion, Brother Juniper. Until he was thirty-five, he spent most of his time in the classroom—first as a student of theology and then as a professor. He also became famous for his preaching. Suddenly he gave it all up and followed the yearning that had begun years before when he heard about the missionary work of St. Francis Solano in South America. Junipero's desire was to convert native peoples in the New World.

Though his feast day is celebrated on July 1 in the United States, it is observed on August 28 throughout the rest of the world.

Arriving by ship at Vera Cruz, Mexico, he and a companion walked the 250 miles to Mexico City. On the way Junipero's left leg became infected by an insect bite, and this would remain a cross—sometimes life-threatening—for the rest of his life. For eighteen years, he worked in central Mexico and in the Baja Peninsula. He became president of the missions there.

Enter politics: the threat of a Russian invasion south from Alaska. Charles III of Spain ordered an expedition to beat Russia to the territory. So the last two conquistadors—one military, one spiritual—began their quest. José de Galvez persuaded Junipero to set out with him for present-day Monterey, California. The first mission founded after the nine-hundred-mile journey north was San Diego in 1769. That year a shortage of food almost canceled the expedition. Vowing to stay with the local people, Junipero and another friar began a novena in preparation for St. Joseph's Day, March 19, the scheduled day of departure. On that day, the relief ship arrived.

Other missions followed: Monterey/Carmel (1770); San Antonio and San Gabriel (1771); San Luís Obispo (1772); San Francisco and San Juan Capistrano (1776); Santa Clara (1777); San Buenaventura (1782). Twelve more were founded after Serra's death.

Junipero made the long trip to Mexico City to settle great differences with the military commander. He arrived at the point of death. The outcome was substantially what Junipero sought: the famous "Regulation" protecting the Indians and the missions. It was the basis for the first significant legislation in California, a "Bill of Rights" for Native Americans.

From the Spanish point of view, the Native Americans were living a "nonhuman" life, so the friars were made their legal guardians. The Native Americans were kept at the mission after Baptism lest they be "corrupted" in their former haunts—a move now regarded by many as unjust treatment.

Junipero's missionary life was a long battle with cold and hunger, with unsympathetic military commanders and even with danger of death from native peoples. Through it all his unquenchable zeal was fed by prayer each night, often from midnight until dawn. He baptized over six thousand people and confirmed five thousand.

He brought the Native Americans not only the gift of faith but also a decent standard of living. He won their love, as witnessed especially by their grief at his death. He is buried at Mission San Carlo Borromeo, Carmel, and was beatified in 1988. Pope Francis canonized him in Washington, DC, on September 23, 2015.

What is a cross you have carried—either physically, emotionally, or spiritually—and how do you deal with it?

....

....

....

....

....

....

....

....

....

For the next nine days, pray a novena for an issue that is important to you, such as peace, equality, or healing. A variety of novenas can be found online.

....

....

....

....

....

....

....

....

....

....

For some, Serra is a challenging individual because of his work to convert Native Americans. Who are some individuals you find challenging in your life? What is it about them that is challenging? Think about what you could do to address that challenge.

....

....

....

....

....

....

....

....

....

....

....

When we pray, the voice of the heart must be heard more than proceedings from the mouth.

St. Bonaventure

St. Bonaventure played an important role in both the medieval Church and the history of the Franciscan Order. A senior faculty member at the University of Paris, St. Bonaventure captured the minds of his students through his academic skills and insights. But more importantly, he captured their hearts through his Franciscan love for Jesus and the Church. For Bonaventure, as for St. Francis, Jesus was the center of everything—his teaching, his administration, his writing, and his life—so much so that he was given the title "Seraphic Doctor."

Born in Bagnorea in 1221, he was baptized John, but received the name Bonaventure when he became a Franciscan at the age of twenty-two. Little is known about his childhood, but we do know that his parents were Giovanni di Fidanza and Maria Ritell. It seems that his father was a physician and a man of means. While St. Francis died about five years after Bonaventure's birth, he is credited with healing the boy of a serious illness.

We celebrate St. Bonaventure's feast on July 15, the day of his death.

St. Bonaventure's teaching career came to a halt when the friars elected him to serve as their General Minister. His seventeen years of service were not easy; the Order was embroiled in conflicts over the interpretation of poverty. Some friars even ended up in heresy, saying that St. Francis and his community were inaugurating the era of the Holy Spirit, which was to replace Jesus, the Church, and Scripture. But because he was a man of prayer and a good administrator, St. Bonaventure managed to structure the Order through effective legislation. But more importantly, he offered the friars an organized spirituality based on the vision and insights of St. Francis. Always a Franciscan at heart and a mystical writer, Bonaventure managed to unite the pastoral, practical aspects of life with the doctrines of the Church. There is a noticeable warmth to his teachings and writings that make him very appealing.

Shortly before Bonaventure ended his service as General Minister, Pope Gregory X made him a cardinal and appointed him bishop of Albano. But a little over a year later, while participating in the Second Council of Lyon, St. Bonaventure died suddenly on July 15, 1274. There is a theory that he was poisoned.

....

Recall one of your favorite teachers. How did he or she impact your life? If possible, reach out and let them know that they made a difference.

....

....

....

....

....

....

....

....

List the ways that you are a leader.

St. Bonaventure is not a saint who captured the imagination of a widespread audience. Do you ever feel as if your gifts and talents aren't widely known or even appreciated? How does that make you feel?

"Who will teach me what is more agreeable to God, that I may do it?"

St. Kateri Tekakwitha

The blood of martyrs is the seed of saints. Nine years after the Jesuits Isaac Jogues and Jean de Lelande were tomahawked by Iroquois warriors, a baby girl was born near the place of their martyrdom, Auriesville, New York.

Her mother was a Christian Algonquin, taken captive by the Iroquois and given as wife to the chief of the Mohawk clan, the boldest and fiercest of the Five Nations. When she was four, Tekakwitha lost her parents and little brother in a smallpox epidemic that left her disfigured and half blind. She was adopted by an uncle, who succeeded her father as chief. He hated the coming of the Blackrobes—Jesuit missionaries—but could do nothing to them because a peace treaty with the French required their presence in villages with Christian captives. She was moved by the words of three Blackrobes who lodged with her uncle, but fear of him kept her from seeking instruction. Tekakwitha refused to marry a Mohawk brave, and at nineteen she finally got the courage to take the step of converting. She was baptized with the name Kateri—Catherine—on Easter Sunday.

St. Kateri's feast day is celebrated on July 14 in the United States and April 17 elsewhere.

Now she would be treated as a slave. Because she would not work on Sunday, Kateri received no food that day. Her life in grace grew rapidly. She told a missionary that she often meditated on the great dignity of being baptized. She was powerfully moved by God's love for human beings and saw the dignity of each of her people.

She was always in danger, for her conversion and holy life created great opposition. On the advice of a priest, Kateri stole away one night and began a two-hundred-mile walking journey to a Christian Indian village at Sault St. Louis, near Montreal.

For three years she grew in holiness under the direction of a priest and an older Iroquois woman, giving herself totally to God in long hours of prayer, in charity, and in strenuous penance. At twenty-three, Kateri took a vow of virginity, an unprecedented act for an Indian woman whose future depended on being married. She found a place in the woods where she could pray an hour a day—and was accused of meeting a man there!

Her dedication to virginity was instinctive: Kateri did not know about religious life for women until she visited Montreal. Inspired by this, she and two friends wanted to start a community, but the local priest dissuaded her. She humbly accepted an "ordinary" life. She practiced severe fasting as penance for the conversion of her nation. Kateri Tekakwitha died the afternoon before Holy Thursday. Witnesses said that her emaciated face changed color and became like that of a healthy child. The lines of suffering, even the pockmarks, disappeared and the touch of a smile appeared on her lips. She was beatified in 1980 and canonized in 2012.

Spend some time in nature and revel in its greatness and beauty. Sit in silence and pray. Or take this journal with you and reflect on the following questions.

....

What about nature seems to foster peace?

....

....

....

....

....

....

....

....

....

What are some qualities of St. Kateri that you admire?

....

....

....

....

....

....

....

....

....

....

Kateri's experience of spiritual direction encouraged her
growth in prayer. How might something similar work for
you?

....

....

....

....

....

....

....

....

....

....

....

....

....

....

....

....

....

....

"I have seen the Lord."

St. Mary Magdalene

Except for the mother of Jesus, few women are more honored in the Bible than Mary Magdalene. Yet she could well be the patron of the slandered, since there has been a persistent legend in the Church that she is the unnamed sinful woman who anointed the feet of Jesus in Luke 7:36–50.

Most Scripture scholars today point out that there is no scriptural basis for confusing the two women. Mary Magdalene—that is, "of Magdala"—was the one from whom Christ cast out "seven demons" (Luke 8:2)—an indication of demonic possession or possibly severe illness.

Writing in the *New Catholic Commentary*, Father Wilfrid J. Harrington, OP, says that "seven demons … does not mean that Mary had lived an immoral life—a conclusion reached only by means of a mistaken identification with the anonymous woman of Luke 7:36." In the *Jerome Biblical Commentary*, Fr. Edward Mally, SJ, agrees that she "is not … the same as the sinner of Luke 7:37, despite the later Western romantic tradition about her."

On July 22, we celebrate the feast of St. Mary Magdalene. She is the patron saint of penitents and perfumers.

Mary Magdalene was one of the many "who were assisting them [Jesus and the Twelve] out of their means." She was one of those who stood by the cross of Jesus with his mother. And of all the "official" witnesses who might have been chosen for the first awareness of the Resurrection, she was the one to whom that privilege was given. She is known as the "Apostle to the Apostles."

....

Is there a time when you were accused of something you did not do? What was your reaction?

....

....

....

....

....

....

....

....

....

....

....

....

....

....

Do you engage in gossip or spread things you know are untrue? Why do you think you do that, even if you know it's wrong?

Even though we know that Mary Magdalene is not the sinful woman she was confused with, why do you think people still do not seem to see her for the important role she played in Jesus' life and ministry?

....

....

....

....

....

....

....

....

....

....

....

....

....

....

....

....

"Trust in God; trust in God."

Bl. Solanus Casey

Barney Casey became one of Detroit's best-known priests even though he was not allowed to preach formally or hear confessions!

Barney came from a large family in Oak Grove, Wisconsin. At the age of twenty-one, and after he had worked as a logger, a hospital orderly, a streetcar operator, and a prison guard, he entered St. Francis Seminary in Milwaukee—where he found the studies difficult. He left there, and in 1896, joined the Capuchins in Detroit, taking the name Solanus. His studies for the priesthood were again arduous.

On July 24, 1904, Solanus was ordained, but because his knowledge of theology was judged to be weak, he was not given permission to hear confessions or to preach. A Franciscan Capuchin who knew him well said this annoying restriction "brought forth in him a greatness and a holiness that might never have been realized in any other way."

Br. Solanus's feast day is July 30, the day before he died.

During his fourteen years as porter and sacristan in Yonkers, New York, Solanus was recognized by the people as a fine speaker. James Derum, his biographer, writes, "For, though he was forbidden to deliver doctrinal sermons, he could give inspirational talks, or feverinos, as the Capuchins termed them." His spiritual fire deeply impressed his listeners.

Fr. Solanus served at parishes in Manhattan and Harlem before returning to Detroit, where he was porter and sacristan for twenty years at St. Bonaventure Monastery. Every Wednesday afternoon, he conducted well-attended services for the sick. A coworker estimates that on the average day 150 to two hundred people came to see Fr. Solanus in the front office. Most of them came to receive his blessing; forty to fifty came for consultation. Many people considered him instrumental in the cures and other blessings they received.

Fr. Solanus' sense of God's providence inspired many of his visitors. "Blessed be God in all his designs" was one of his favorite expressions.

The many friends of Fr. Solanus helped the Capuchins to begin a soup kitchen during the Depression. Capuchins are still feeding the hungry there today.

In failing health, Solanus was transferred to the Capuchin novitiate in Huntington, Indiana, in 1946, where he lived for ten years until needing to be hospitalized in Detroit. Fr. Solanus died on July 31, 1957. An estimated twenty thousand people passed by his coffin before his burial in St. Bonaventure Church in Detroit.

At the funeral Mass, the provincial Fr. Gerald said: "His was a life of service and love for people like me and you. When he was not himself sick, he nevertheless suffered with and for you that were sick. When he was not physically hungry, he hungered with people like you. He had a divine love for people. He loved people for what he could do for them—and for God, through them."

In 1960, a Father Solanus Guild was formed in Detroit to aid Capuchin seminarians. By 1967, the guild had five thousand members—many of them grateful recipients of his practical advice and his comforting assurance that God would not abandon them in their trials. Solanus Casey was declared Venerable in 1995 and beatified on November 18, 2017.

....

If Solanus Casey demonstrated anything, it's that holiness can be found in the simplest of actions, such as just listening or talking to people. How would you describe holiness?

....

....

....

....

....

....

....

....

Bl. Solanus is a great example that there are many avenues and ways one can be a witness to people. He was not allowed to preach or hear confessions, but in his work as a porter and sacristan, he still ministered to many. In your life, what are some avenues that offer you a chance to serve others?

....

....

....

....

....

....

....

....

....

....

....

Has there been a time that someone underestimated your abilities to do something? What was your reaction?

....

....

....

....

....

....

....

....

....

....

....

"Even if the world were to capsize, if everything were to become dark, hazy, tumultuous, God would still be with us."

St. Padre Pio

••

In one of the largest such ceremonies in history, Pope John Paul II canonized Padre Pio of Pietrelcina on June 16, 2002. More than 300,000 people braved blistering heat as they filled St. Peter's Square and nearby streets. They heard the Holy Father praise the new saint for his prayer and charity. "This is the most concrete synthesis of Padre Pio's teaching," said the pope. He also stressed Padre Pio's witness to the power of suffering. If accepted with love, the Holy Father stressed, such suffering can lead to "a privileged path of sanctity."

Many people have turned to the Italian Capuchin Franciscan to intercede with God on their behalf; among them was the future Pope John Paul II. In 1962, when he was still an archbishop in Poland, he wrote to Padre Pio and asked him to pray for a Polish woman with throat cancer. Within two weeks, she had been cured of her life-threatening disease.

St. Padre Pio's feast day is September 23. He is the patron saint of stress relief and adolescents.

Born Francesco Forgione, Padre Pio grew up in a family of farmers in southern Italy. Twice his father worked in Jamaica, New York, to provide the family income.

At the age of fifteen, Francesco joined the Capuchins and took the name of Pio. He was ordained in 1910 and drafted during World War I. After he was discovered to have tuberculosis, he was discharged.

In 1917, he was assigned to the friary in San Giovanni Rotondo, seventy-five miles from the city of Bari on the Adriatic.

On September 20, 1918, as he was making his thanksgiving after Mass, Padre Pio had a vision of Jesus. When the vision ended, he had the stigmata in his hands, feet, and side.

Life became more complicated after that. Medical doctors, Church authorities, and curiosity seekers came to see Padre Pio. In 1924, and again in 1931, the authenticity of the stigmata was questioned; Padre Pio was not permitted to celebrate Mass publicly or to hear confessions. He did not complain of these decisions, which were soon reversed. However, he wrote no letters after 1924. His only other writing, a pamphlet on the agony of Jesus, was done before 1924.

Padre Pio rarely left the friary after he received the stigmata, but busloads of people soon began coming to see him. Each morning after a 5:00 a.m. Mass in a crowded church, he heard confessions until noon. He took a mid-morning break to bless the sick and all who came to see him. Every afternoon he also heard confessions. In time his confessional ministry would take ten hours a day; penitents had to take a number so that the situation could be handled. Many of them have said that Padre Pio knew details of their lives they had never mentioned.

Padre Pio saw Jesus in all the sick and suffering. At his urging, a fine hospital was built on nearby Mount Gargano. The idea arose in 1940, and a committee began to collect money. Ground was broken in 1946. Building the hospital was a technical wonder because of the difficulty of getting water there and of hauling up the building supplies. This "House for the Alleviation of Suffering" has 350 beds.

A number of people have reported cures they believe were received through the intercession of Padre Pio. Those who assisted at his Masses came away edified; several curiosity seekers were deeply moved. Like St. Francis, Padre Pio sometimes had his habit torn or cut by souvenir hunters.

One of Padre Pio's sufferings was that unscrupulous people several times circulated prophecies that they claimed originated from him. He never made prophecies about world events and never gave an opinion on matters that he felt belonged to Church authorities to decide. He died on September 23, 1968, and was beatified in 1999.

Think about a time in your life when you have suffered. What did you learn from that experience?

....

....

....

....

....

....

If you were to encounter Padre Pio and witness his stigmata, what would your reaction be?

....

....

....

....

....

....

....

....

....

Padre Pio encountered a lot of doubters in his life,
something to which we can probably all relate. If there was a
time that others didn't believe you about something, how did
it make you feel?

....

....

....

....

....

....

....

....

....

....

....

"All people are born as originals but many die as photocopies"

Bl. Carlo Acutis

....

Born in London and raised in Milan, Carlo's wealthy parents were not particularly religious. Upon receiving his first communion at age seven, Carlo became a frequent communicant, making a point of praying before the tabernacle before or after every Mass. In addition to Francis of Assisi, Carlo took several of the younger saints as his models, including Bernadette Soubirous, Jacinta and Francisco Marto, and Dominic Savio.

At school Carlo tried to comfort friends whose parents were undergoing divorce, as well as stepping in to defend disabled students from bullies. After school hours, he volunteered his time with the city's homeless and destitute. Considered a computer geek by some, Carlo spent four years creating a website dedicated to cataloguing every reported Eucharistic miracle around the world. He also enjoyed films, comics, soccer, and playing popular video games.

The feast day of Bl. Carlo Acutis is October 12, the day of his death.

Diagnosed with leukemia, Carlo offered his sufferings to God for the intentions of the sitting pope—Benedict XVI—and the entire Church. His longtime desire to visit as many sites of Eucharistic miracles as possible was cut short by his illness. Carlo died in 2006 and was beatified in 2020. As he had wished, Carlo was buried in Assisi at St. Mary Major's "Chapel of the Stripping," where Francis had returned his clothes to his father and began a more radical following of the Gospel.

Among the thousands present for Carlo's beatification at Assisi's Basilica of St. Francis were many of his childhood friends. Presiding at the beatification service, Cardinal Agostino Vallini praised Carlo as an example of how young people can use technology to spread the Gospel "to reach as many people as possible and help them know the beauty of friendship with the Lord." His liturgical feast is celebrated on October 12.

Carlo Acutis probably never imagined that what he was doing during his life would eventually put him on the path to sainthood. What types of skills do you have that could raise up the Church and the faith of others?

Take some time and reflect on how you use technology and social media. Does your online behavior add to the positivity or negativity of the world? Now, write down ways you can use social media to encourage others or bring joy to the world. Put those ideas into action.

If someone were to write an entry about your life similar to
this one about Carlo, what would you want it to say?

"God will not ask us how eloquently we have spoken, but how well we have lived."

Venerable Matt Talbot

Matt can be considered the patron of men and women struggling with alcoholism. He was born in Dublin, where his father worked on the docks and had a difficult time supporting his family. After a few years of schooling, Matt obtained work as a messenger for some liquor merchants; there he began to drink excessively. For fifteen years—until he was almost thirty—Matt was an active alcoholic.

One day he decided to take "the pledge" for three months, make a general confession, and begin to attend daily Mass. There is evidence that Matt's first seven years after taking the pledge were especially difficult. Avoiding his former drinking places was hard. He began to pray as intensely as he used to drink. He also tried to pay back people from whom he had borrowed or stolen money while he was drinking.

Venerable Matt Talbot's feast day is June 19. He is the patron saint of sobriety.

Most of his life, Matt worked as a builder's laborer. He joined the Secular Franciscan Order and began a life of strict penance; he abstained from meat nine months a year. Matt spent hours every night avidly reading Scripture and the lives of the saints. He prayed the Rosary conscientiously. Though his job did not make him rich, Matt contributed generously to the missions.

After 1923, Matt's health failed, and he was forced to quit work. He died on his way to church on Trinity Sunday. Fifty years later, Pope

Paul VI gave Matt Talbot the title Venerable. His liturgical feast is celebrated on June 19.

....

Not everyone is addicted to alcohol like Talbot was. People may, however, have other addictions, such as to drugs, cigarettes, food, gambling, and so on. Addictions can be big or small. We can be addicted to our phones, video games, work, or shopping. The first step is to acknowledge that we are struggling with something that seems to be out of our control. Reflect on what you think you might have an addiction to and identify ways you can address it.

Write down some of the blessings you receive from the work that you do. Perhaps you are helping others with your job, or you are working to create something for the benefit of society. Whatever it is, recognize that what you are doing is important.

A lot of times, people can have rather negative views of those struggling with addiction. Take some time to really think about how you express your feelings about this topic. Do you tend to be judgmental or understanding?

"A single act of humility is worth more than the proud exhibition of any virtue."

St. Frances Xavier Cabrini

Frances Xavier Cabrini was the first United States citizen to be canonized. Her deep trust in the loving care of her God gave her the strength to be a valiant woman doing the work of Christ.

Refused admission to the religious order that had educated her to be a teacher, she began charitable work at the House of Providence Orphanage in Cadogno, Italy. In September 1877, she made her vows there.

When the bishop closed the orphanage in 1880, he named Frances prioress of the Missionary Sisters of the Sacred Heart. Seven young women from the orphanage joined her.

St. Frances's feast day is November 13. She is the patron saint of immigrants and impossible causes.

Since her early childhood in Italy, Frances had wanted to be a missionary in China but, at the urging of Pope Leo XIII, Frances went west instead of east. She traveled with six sisters to New York City to work with the thousands of Italian immigrants living there.

She found disappointment and difficulties with every step. When she arrived in New York, the house intended to be her first orphanage in the United States was not available. The archbishop advised her to return to Italy. But Frances, truly a valiant woman, departed from the archbishop's residence all the more determined to establish that orphanage. And she did.

In thirty-five years, Frances Xavier Cabrini founded sixty-seven institutions dedicated to caring for the poor, the abandoned, the uneducated, and the sick. Seeing great need among Italian immigrants who were losing their faith, she organized schools and adult education classes.

As a child, she was always frightened of water, unable to overcome her fear of drowning. Yet despite this fear, she traveled across the Atlantic Ocean more than thirty times. She died of malaria in her own Columbus Hospital in Chicago.

Everyone has experienced some type of rejection or disappointment. When it happened to you, were you inspired to try harder, or did you let it defeat you?

....

**Identify some of your fears and think about how you can
face them.**

....

....

....

....

....

....

....

....

....

....

....

....

....

....

....

....

....

....

....

....

What are some ways you can emulate this saint?

....

....

....

....

....

....

....

....

....

....

....

....

....

....

....

....

....

"It is not necessary to teach others, to cure them or to improve them; it is only necessary to live among them, sharing the human condition and being present to them in love."

Bl. Charles de Foucauld

Born into an aristocratic family in Strasbourg, France, Charles was orphaned at the age of six and raised by his devout grandfather. He rejected the Catholic faith as a teenager and joined the French army. Inheriting a great deal of money from his grandfather, Charles went to Algeria with his regiment, but not without his mistress, Mimi.

When he refused to give her up, he was dismissed from the army. Still in Algeria, he left Mimi and reenlisted in the army. Denied permission to make a scientific exploration of nearby Morocco, he resigned from the service. With the help of a Jewish rabbi, Charles disguised himself as a Jew and in 1883, he began a one-year exploration, which he recorded in a book that was well received.

Bl. Charles' feast day is December 1, marking the day of his death.

Inspired by the Jews and Muslims whom he met, Charles resumed the practice of his Catholic faith when he returned to France in 1886. He joined a Trappist monastery in Ardeche, France, and later transferred to one in Akbes, Syria. Leaving the monastery in 1897, Charles worked as gardener and sacristan for the Poor Clare nuns in Nazareth and later in Jerusalem. In 1901, he returned to France and was ordained a priest.

Later that year, Charles journeyed to Beni-Abbes, Morocco, intending to found a monastic religious community in North Africa that offered hospitality to Christians, Muslims, Jews, or people with no religion. He lived a peaceful, hidden life but attracted no companions.

A former army comrade invited him to live among the Tuareg people in Algeria. Charles learned their language enough to write a Tuareg-French and French-Tuareg dictionary and translate the Gospels into Tuareg. In 1905, he came to Tamanrasset, where he lived the rest of his life. A two-volume collection of Charles' Tuareg poetry was published after his death.

In early 1909, he visited France and established an association of laypeople who pledged to live by the Gospels. His return to Tamanrasset was welcomed by the Tuareg. In 1915, Charles wrote to Louis Massignon: "The love of God, the love for one's neighbor.... All religion is found there.... How to get to that point? Not in a day since it is perfection itself: it is the goal we must always aim for, which we must unceasingly try to reach and that we will only attain in heaven."

The outbreak of World War I led to attacks on the French in Algeria. Seized in a raid by another tribe, Charles and two French soldiers visiting him were shot to death on December 1, 1916.

Five religious congregations, associations, and spiritual institutes—Little Brothers of Jesus, Little Sisters of the Sacred Heart, Little Sisters of Jesus, Little Brothers of the Gospel, and Little Sisters of the Gospel—all draw inspiration from the peaceful, largely hidden, yet hospitable life that characterized Charles. He was beatified on November 13, 2005.

Have you ever struggled with your faith or even stepped away from it for a while, like Charles did? What caused you to do so? What brought you back?

....
....
....
....
....
....
....
....
....
....

Given his connection with many different faiths, Charles seems a great inspiration to engage in interreligious dialogue. Make a list of questions you would have for members of various faiths and try to find a way to get them answered. After all, knowledge is powerful.

....
....
....
....

....

....

....

....

....

....

Charles seemed to have many adventures. What are the adventures you've been on and what did you learn from them? What are your plans for future adventures?

....

....

....

....

....

....

....

....

....

....

....

....

"True wisdom, then, consists in works, not in great talents."

St. Bridget of Sweden

From age seven on, Bridget had visions of Christ crucified. Her visions formed the basis for her activity—always with the emphasis on charity rather than spiritual favors.

She lived her married life in the court of Swedish King Magnus II. Mother of eight children—the second eldest was St. Catherine of Sweden—Bridget lived the strict life of a penitent after her husband's death.

Bridget constantly strove to exert her good influence over Magnus; while never fully reforming, he did give her land and buildings to found a monastery for men and women. This group eventually expanded into an Order known as the Bridgetines.

In 1350, a year of jubilee, Bridget braved a plague-stricken Europe to make a pilgrimage to Rome. Although she never returned to Sweden, her years in Rome were far from happy, as she was hounded by debts and by opposition to her work against Church abuses.

The feast day of St. Bridget is July 23, the day of her death in 1373. She is the patron saint of Europe.

A final pilgrimage to the Holy Land, marred by shipwreck and the death of her son, Charles, eventually led to her death in 1373. In 1999, St. Bridget, St. Catherine of Siena, and St. Teresa Benedicta of the Cross, were named co-patronesses of Europe.

St. Bridget made a number of pilgrimages in her life. If you were to make a pilgrimage, where would you go? Why would you choose that place?

This saint took an interest in the many issues of her time. What are some issues that resonate with you and why?

The story of St. Bridget seems very relatable in a lot of ways. She was a wife and mother. Yet she is a saint. What do you think makes a saint?

"Sometimes we so much occupy ourselves with trying to live like angels that we neglect to be good men and women."

St. Francis de Sales

....

Francis was destined by his father to be a lawyer so the young man could eventually take his elder's place as a senator from the province of Savoy in France. For this reason, Francis was sent to Padua to study law. After receiving his doctorate, he returned home and, in due time, told his parents he wished to enter the priesthood. His father strongly opposed Francis in this, and only after much patient persuasiveness on the part of the gentle Francis did his father finally consent. Francis was ordained and elected provost of the Diocese of Geneva, then a center for the Calvinists. Francis set out to convert them, especially in the district of Chablais. By preaching and distributing the little pamphlets he wrote to explain true Catholic doctrine, he had remarkable success.

At age thirty-five, he became bishop of Geneva. While administering his diocese he continued to preach, hear confessions, and catechize the children. His gentle character was a great asset in winning souls. He practiced his own axiom, "A spoonful of honey attracts more flies than a barrelful of vinegar."

The feast of St. Francis de Sales is January 24. He is the patron saint of authors and deafness.

Besides his two well-known books, *The Introduction to the Devout Life* and *A Treatise on the Love of God*, he wrote many pamphlets and carried on a vast correspondence. For his writings, he has been named patron of the Catholic Press. His writings, filled with his characteristic humble spirit, are addressed to laypeople. He wanted to make them understand that they, too, are called to be saints. As he wrote in *The Introduction to the Devout Life*: "It is an error, or rather a heresy, to say devotion is incompatible with the life of a soldier, a tradesman, a prince, or a married woman.... It has happened that many have lost perfection in the desert who had preserved it in the world."

In spite of his busy and comparatively short life, he had time to collaborate with another saint, Jane Frances de Chantal, in the work of establishing the Sisters of the Visitation. These women were to practice the virtues exemplified in Mary's visit to Elizabeth: humility, piety, and mutual charity. At first they engaged in limited works of mercy for the poor and the sick. Today, while some communities conduct schools, others live a strictly contemplative life.

....

Words can be powerful. Take time to go back and read some of your previous writings in this journal. In doing so, you may be inspired to write more on that entry or simply pray and reflect on what you have written.

....

....

....

....

....

....

....

....

St. Francis wanted laypeople to realize that they, too, are called to be saints. In what ways do you consider yourself holy and saintly? Try to remember that, at some point, these saints were ordinary persons just like each of us.

St. Francis' life is a reminder that each of us must follow our own paths. What has your journey looked like thus far and where do you see it going in the future?

About the Author

Susan Hines-Brigger has been writing her entire life. She is an executive editor of *St. Anthony Messenger*, for which she has written the "Faith and Family" column for over twenty years. She has also written many of Franciscan Media's seasonal devotional booklets. She lives in Cincinnati, Ohio, with her husband and four children.